MORE

LESSONS LEARNED

FROM OUR

MISTAKES

Michael Rosman

www.TheCorporateCaterer.com

ISBN-13: 978-0692655610 (Corporate Caterer, The)
ISBN-10: 0692655611

DEDICATION

"There's a simple doctrine: outside of a person's love, the most sacred thing that they can give is their labor. And somehow or another along the way, we tend to forget that. Labor is a very precious thing that you have. Anytime that you can combine labor with love, you've made a good merger."

-James Carville, Political Strategist
Presidential Election Eve
November, 1992

More *Lessons Learned from Our Mistakes* is dedicated to the exceptionally talented and creative individuals who have contributed their precious labor, and whose influence and clout has opened doors during the evolution of The Corporate Caterer. Someone once said, "The Road to Success is Always under Construction." I am grateful to be travelling that road with these people:

Nathan Havey, Jay Mantri, Kristina Pelletier, Michael Attias, Rose Abao, Fan Stanbrough, Michael Stanbrough, Elizabeth Appleby, Kathryn Frankson, Linda West, Carl Sacks, Kathleen Stoehr, Jack Milan, Meryl Snow, Anina Kostecki, Sam Radbil, Richard Radbil, and Christine Bevilacqua.

ACKNOWLEGMENT

Richard Radbil is a colleague who owned and operated a very successful corporate catering business in Wisconsin for 30 years. Today, he is happily retired from the industry. However, like most of us, the food business remains in his blood. Richard has graciously collaborated on some of the content in these pages.

The quotes throughout the book are a compilation from: *The Harvard Business Review, Forbes, Entrepreneur and Michael Rosman*

PREFACE

The Gateway

Please visit TheCorporateCaterer.com for free downloads and information about our membership services. Our multimedia website shares behind-the-scenes tips, customizable templates and menus, checklists and worksheets, sample sales scripts, videos, recorded conferences, and how-to resources for operating a financially successful corporate drop-off/delivery catering business.

Whether you are just getting started in this segment of the industry or a seasoned veteran, our membership website offers an enormous amount of invaluable information.

Additionally, we offer individual teleconferencing **Coaching Membership Packages** and custom on-site **Consulting Services**. From creating a corporate menu to strategizing a step-by-step plan to take your corporate division to the next level, we are a team of industry experts ready to assist you.

I am often asked if we "have lists." The answer is, "No, we have something much better." Members have access to our pioneering **Leads Program.** This is how it works:

(1) You give us zip codes where you want to go after new business.

(2) Our specially trained in-house lead generators make hundreds of cold calls on your behalf.

(3) You receive a confidential file of prequalified companies that order catering regularly with all the pertinent contact information.

For more details, visit,

www.TheCorporateCaterer.com and click the **ADDITIONAL SERVICES** link at the top of the homepage. If you would like to speak to Michael directly or even schedule a complementary consultation to discuss your businesses goals, please call our corporate office at 781-641-3303.

INTRODUCTION

The first volume of *Lessons Learned from Our Mistakes* contains 50 real-life screw-ups, ill-conceived game plans, and wrong decisions (that felt right at the time) from my 30-plus years in the industry. Most importantly, it shares the lessons learned from these experiences and offers strategies you can apply to your own operation.

MORE *Lessons Learned From Our Mistakes* shares the same message in spirit; however, it is formatted in a more narrative style and includes pieces of my personal and professional journey. I share a wide-ranging compilation of experiences from three decades in the catering battlefield. I hope they help you navigate the sometimes choppy waters of this crazy business.

As was our message in volume #1, "Let our pain be your gain!"

The 2015 IBIS report for Caterers in the US is *very* encouraging. Not only has total revenue increased to $12 billion annually, but the corporate drop-off segment now accounts for over 25% of the industry. If you are not part of this sector, the time for entry is ripe. If you have a corporate drop-off division and would like to take it to the next level, we welcome you—you've come to the right place!

1987-1991:

My Professional Road Traveled

As a wet-behind-the-ears 20-something know-it-all, I was accepted in a management training program with a leading, innovative food service company in Boston. One year of front-of-the-house, back-of-the-house, and kitchen training was an invigorating eye-opener and taught me that I knew practically nothing about the industry.

After completing the program, I spent the next four years working at different catering and food service venues throughout the company. Along the way, I learned a lot, screwed up some, and figured out that I liked what I was doing—most days.

1991–1995:

The Sink or Swim (or Both) Years

Realizing a goal I had been working towards, I signed a purchase and sale agreement on an existing breakfast and lunch restaurant in the financial district on Boston's prestigious Beacon Hill. I liked the concept of working

Monday through Friday, with no nights and no weekends. However, I soon discovered that nights and weekends were spent finishing the work I couldn't get to during the week.

The next five years were spent running the restaurant and trying to build a corporate catering division. Our kitchen prep space was approximately the size of a small jail cell, which got particularly challenging when we actually started generating some catering business. While I had some experience at this point (in retrospect, not very much), there was a fair amount of learning as I went along. I remember often feeling like I had woken up in an unfamiliar house in the middle of the night, patting along the walls for a light switch.

A pizzeria operated one floor above my restaurant. About three years into my tenancy, Mario, the owner, decided he'd had enough. One summer night, he took his pizza paddles and disappeared. Due to the unique lease situation I had gotten myself into (if I only knew then the things I know now. . .), I, as the primary leaseholder of both restaurants, now owned a pizzeria.

For the record, my previous pizzeria experience consisted of popping a frozen Celeste Pizza-for-

One (Four Cheese) in the oven. Looking back, I can now spin this as a glass half-full, behind-every-cloud-is-a-silver-lining event.

Two things happened right away:

(1) We added an Italian-themed 50-item salad bar, which was a big hit (while on the topic, where have all the salad bars gone from restaurants? I miss them); and

(2) We gained much-needed workspace for the growing catering business. Since the pizzeria didn't open until 11:00 a.m., our morning production area went from the jail cell to the second floor penthouse. We were movin' on up.

I *could* say that I eventually learned to spin a helluva pizza, but that would be a stretch. Maybe I made a decent one, but that's it.

During this time, I learned **a lot** about starting and building a corporate catering business out of an operating restaurant(s). I also absorbed a fair amount of learning-as-you-go bumps and bruises along the way.

As it turned out, these five years of *growth opportunity*, a term I use to describe learning from mistakes, were invaluable down the road.

1996:

The Earliest (and Shortest) Retirement on Record

My first five-year lease (a mistake; it's not long enough) was coming up for renewal, and I had a decision to make. The restaurants were doing OK. I was working a ton of hours, paying the bills, and earning a modest salary. The catering business was starting to take off, just not as rapidly as my rent(s).

I quickly discovered that with more business, I needed more staff, equipment, delivery vehicles, and more of everything, especially working capital. Because I was now paying rent on two restaurants, I tried renegotiating with the landlord, a tough older Sicilian man named Sal. He came in for breakfast every morning impeccably dressed, with never a hair out of place—very old school. His only response was, "No, no, no, cannot lower rent. You a smart guy. You'll figure out."

What I figured out was that operating what was quickly becoming more of a catering business at a high profile location didn't make sense. Because my passion for corporate catering was overtaking my desire to run restaurants, I decided it was time to find a less expensive location that was set up better for catering.

Easier said than done.

I probably looked at a dozen places, but could not find what I was looking for. My time window was closing, and I had to figure something out—fast. In what I would call a combination of panic, intestinal fortitude, and creativity, I opened up the Yellow Pages (pre-Internet) and started calling other catering companies in the area. After tracking down the owner/right person to speak to, the conversation would begin something like this:

> Hi, [fill in name], I am a competitor of yours (introduce myself). My lease is about to expire, and I'm not renewing it. I'm actively looking for a new location, but haven't found one yet. I am wondering if you would have any desire to rent me some temporary space in your kitchen where we could operate until I find a new home.

The typical response was "Umm . . . ahh . . . ok . . . umm . . . ahh . . . what did you say your name was?"

It was an interesting time.

Over the next few weeks, I met with about a half dozen of my competitors and potential temporary landlords. We would start out discussing how a transitory lease situation would work. Inevitably, each meeting would reveal more of the many questions that such a unique situation would present, including the following:

- *How are two competitors going to successfully share the same space?*

- *What are the chances of both teams of employees working in harmony?*

- *What about the phones?*

- *Isn't it going to be a little dicey regarding proprietary issues, such as operational structures and competition for each other's customers and recipes?*

And on it went. Then something happened.

I was meeting with the owner of an independent, large volume operation in the heart of the downtown financial district. He had an excellent reputation, and I'd always admired the business that he had built. After doing the usual dance for about 20 minutes, he asked, "Why don't you just sell me your client list?"

Hmmm, I thought. *Let's see* . . . I was worried about the clock running out. I had about two weeks before my lease ended, with nowhere to go. I was feeling tired, hassled, and conflicted. Truthfully, I didn't really know what "sell me your client list" meant, but I do remember associating it with me handing him my problem and him handing me a check. We began to discuss and negotiate different ways that an agreement could be structured. After a couple of days of back and forth, we made a deal.

I would receive some up-front money (however, fantasies of buying a private island would remain just that—fantasies) and a percentage of sales from my client list for one year, paid monthly. And, I would spend the next two months working with his company to ensure a smooth transition, which was in both of our interests.

Those two months were a unique and valuable experience. It was fascinating to see the inner workings of a well-oiled operation that generated over $5 million annually in corporate catering revenue. I learned a lot about how one of the big leaguers did it on a day-to-day basis.

Inevitably, issues arose that neither of us had ever dealt with. Integrating both staffs (a hard proposition—a couple of my people were not happy and didn't stick around long), the delicate task of communicating with my customers that we were "merging" (the term I was using) with another caterer, consolidating vendors, and working in an unfamiliar space created new challenges every day.

I had been warned that a big problem could arise soon after I was no longer involved in the day-to-day operations: "Don't be surprised if the monthly checks stopped arriving." I was fortunate. I made a deal with a great operator, who I learned so much from, and he was a principled businessman. He honored our agreement.

1997:

The Next Chapter (or so I thought)

After taking a few months off, it was time to get back to work. The world was my oyster. I was free to pursue any field I wanted. I considered the following:

(1) A career in sports broadcasting

(2) Becoming a private investigator

(3) Being a regular game show contestant and winning enough cash/prizes to comfortably live on.

My first pursuit was sports broadcasting. I learned that I'd have to go to broadcasting school for two years. Then, the school would try to help place me in an entry-level job, which presumably would entail moving to some remote location in, say, Boise, Idaho.

From there, I might get a gig at a local cable channel, calling play-by-play for girls' junior varsity field hockey, making minimum wage. And that was if I was lucky and everything fell into place. It appeared that my plan to become the next voice of the Boston Red Sox was a little further off on the horizon than I realized.

My career as a sports broadcaster was over.

Private investigator sounded cool, with an element of intrigue and danger that had appeal. I actually got an offer from a company. They told me I would have to start at the bottom because I had no experience—sounded reasonable. I was also told that I should not count on making much money for the first couple years—sounded realistic.

I proposed spending a couple days out in the

field with one of the investigators, getting a feel for what the job entailed. They agreed. As prearranged, one morning I met Annie, a senior investigator, at a McDonald's parking lot at 4:00 a.m. We were going on a stakeout.

I got in her car, and we drove about 15 minutes to a residential neighborhood. On the way, she explained that we had been hired to investigate a worker's compensation claim. "Roger," who had injured his back at work, had been collecting disability checks for two years.

He had just filed yet another extension request, asserting he was still in too much pain to work. Annie said that we would wait for him to leave his house, and then we would, in her words, "tail his ass and see how much pain this joker is really in."

She also told me that if I wanted to, I could call her "Agent X." I am not making this up.

It was VERY, VERY exciting—for about 10 minutes. We waited and waited and waited. For **eight hours**, from 4:30 a.m. until 12:30 p.m., we sat in Annie/Agent X's car and did nothing. He never left the house. It was excruciating. On top of it, about every 15 minutes, Annie/Agent X would sing-out, "Ro-o-o-o-ger, come out, come out, wherever you are."

My career as a private investigator was over.

Finally, I decided the answer had been in front of me, literally, the whole time. I had been watching *The Price is Right*, *Wheel of Fortune*, *$25,000 Pyramid*, *Family Feud,* and *Jeopardy* (too hard) for years. One day I woke up said, "Hello!! Is anyone home?? I'll just go on those shows, jump around the stage like a crazy person, and win lots of money!"

While the specific details are sketchy today, after spending a couple of days on the phone gathering information about how it all worked, I clearly remember thinking, "This is what they mean by, *if it sounds too good to be true, it probably is.*"

My career as a career game show contestant was over.

So, after some soul searching and acknowledging that I had the food business in my blood, I decided I'd go back to what I knew and liked, most of the time.

1997–2012

(Round #2)

My first decade in the industry laid the groundwork for the next big challenge. I was offered a position to create corporate catering division for a burgeoning restaurant and full-service caterer in suburban Boston.

It was my home for the next 15 years.

By 1998, my first full year, corporate catering sales were $120,000.

By 2012, we were closing in on $2 million annually.

It was a busy 15 years.

Today—after four major renovations, one fire, three floods, one robbery, about 187 power outages, a dozen or so blown compressors, complete systems crashes, no heat in January, no air-conditioning in July, a fleet of delivery vehicles that require never-ending maintenance—we are a one-hundred seat full-service restaurant and bar and a social and corporate catering company generating almost $5 million annually.

BOSTON, MASSACHUSETTS, 1991

It happened in the blink of an eye.

I answered the phone at my restaurant, just as I had done about a hundred times a day. However, on this day I was asked a question I'd never heard before.

"We're looking for a local restaurant to cater breakfast and lunch every Tuesday and Thursday for the next six months. It'd be for 20 people. We can spend $10 a head for breakfast and $15 for lunch. Is this something you can handle?"

"Ahh . . . yes! Absolutely!" I responded. The fact that I'd never catered a single corporate meal was secondary to the numbers I was furiously pounding into my calculator.

So began my transition from restaurateur to corporate drop-off caterer. Little did I know, that phone call would be the catalyst that transformed a struggling restaurant into a nearly $2-million-a-year flourishing company. The concept of repeat business may not have been a conscious pursuit at the time, but it certainly became one.

Those early years encompassed a lot of trial and error while we found our footing. The most significant lesson learned was the benefit of offering "tastings" as the centerpiece of our sales strategy. Tastings, which involve prearranged, complimentary food samples being delivered to the decision makers of local companies, were the engine that spurred our growth. It appears that the concept of a "free lunch" will never go out of style.

Corporate tastings are a process. They involve acquiring lists of companies, making cold calls, gathering contact information, qualifying potential new clients, sending and emailing menus, scheduling and executing them, and systematically following up.

A well-rounded marketing program also includes a coordinated fusion of social media, regular promotions, in-house merchandising, and professional packaging designed to interlink all of these components.

It's All about the Numbers

After three decades in the trenches, these are some tried-and-true concepts about building a corporate drop-off catering division through tastings:

1) Some of the most universal industries to target are venture capital, consulting, pharmaceutical, life sciences, IT training, law firms, and colleges and universities.

2) It takes about 10 cold calls to get one prospect. (A prospect is a company that orders frequently enough to qualify for a tasting.)

3) It takes about 200 cold calls to schedule 20 tastings.

4) If executed well and followed up systematically, on average, 20 tastings are going to generate 5 new clients (repeat business), 10 new customers (that order periodically), and 5 duds (that never order).

Keep in mind that these figures are variable. There is no magic wand, and there are no absolutes. You may present 20 tastings that convert into 15 clients, but the next round of 20 may generate only 5 clients.

The most overlooked component of the process is follow-up work after the tasting. Shifting prospects' ordering routines can be challenging. Will they be back for more?

Maybe Tomorrow

Consider this scenario: You're in your office at the end of a long day. An email arrives from a new produce company that wants your business. You open the email (maybe) to find an attractive promotional flyer with appealing photos and reasonable price points. You're always on the lookout for better products and pricing, but you're tired and ready to go home. You think, *maybe I'll give them a call tomorrow*. You might, but chances are you won't. It's not that you aren't interested, but as usual, you have a dozen other issues percolating.

This is the equivalent of you emailing or sending a menu to a prospect and sitting by the phone hoping the prospect will call.

What would it take for you to actually place an order with a new produce company? A follow-up call or calls? A representative visiting you—perhaps with some free samples? If you do place an order, chances are very good that it would be due of the company's persistence. It can be challenging to get someone to change their buying habits.

Imagine that you place an order and are pleased. Will you order a second time? Or is it possible that something as insignificant as having to search for the company's phone number or filling out a credit application will stop you? The point is, even after a successful first delivery, the produce company will probably have to continue to court you for your continued business.

Expect the same challenges when you are pursuing new clients. You are an unknown. Ordering from a new vendor can feel like a hassle. It can feel like extra work.

"I have a flawed and incomplete understanding of what it feels like to work for me."

DAVID versus GOLIATH

As a fervent football fan—born, raised, and living in Boston—I have been spoiled by the unprecedented success of my beloved New England Patriots. In pursuit of our fifth championship and seventh Super Bowl appearance this millennium, I recently wondered, "Excluding the six states that comprise New England, why do football fans from the rest of the country enthusiastically root for the demise of my team?"

A local sports columnist recently nailed the answer: "Because nobody roots for Goliath."

Bingo. David versus Goliath . . . the biblical story recounting how a young, physically inferior shepherd rose from obscurity to defeat a mighty warrior.

I follow with a similar question, one I am regularly asked in my line of work: "How does my business (David) compete against the Paneras (Goliaths) of the world?"

For starters, unlike David, it is not necessary (or realistic) to slay the catering Goliaths in your marketplace. There is room for you both.

Should you keep an eye on your competition? Sure, but only to a point. Your primary goal is to build the best business you possibly can, rather than replicate what others are doing. If you see Panera Bread trucks delivering catering in your area, it's a good sign. It means business is out there waiting to be captured. My experience have taught me that the road to success is straighter if you focus on what you do and do it phenomenally.

Is Bigger Really Better?

Panera's 2014 Report to Stockholders stated that its 1,880 locations grossed $2.13 billion, and catering sales figures revealed double-digit growth for the last two years.

QSR magazine estimates that the big six of Chipotle, Panera, Noodles, Qdoba, Potbelly, and Panda Express combine for an estimated $13.2 billion annually in catering sales. Catering is in italics to illustrate a point. It wasn't until 2013 that Chipotle (with revenue almost twice that of Panera's) decided it was time to enter the catering market. After a substantial investment to launch the new division, it appears they stumbled—badly—out of the gate. Apparently, someone forgot to check the definition of catering because what they currently offer is a pickup service.

Today, their website's Catering FAQ page

sheepishly states, "We don't offer delivery right now, but we've gotten the message loud and clear, and this is something we're looking into for catering orders."

Oh, and all Chipotle's orders are COD. Again, from their website:

> Q) *"Can I set up a House Account, PO Number, or be invoiced for catering orders?"*

> A) *"Not yet. We're working on getting a system in place though, stay tuned."*

> The lesson? Bigger does NOT automatically mean better. Goliath is far from perfect.

Leverage Your Independence

Let's start by dispelling the myth that it is safer to do business with large chains because they have systems that ensure a better customer experience. In fact, to boost their bottom line, the Goliaths of the world will sometimes make impactful compromises in both their products and services. A board of directors, made up of people who may have no clue as to what being on the front lines is all about, decides that its company's spreadsheets need to improve.

"Easy," they conclude. "We'll cut back our

portion sizes a bit and trim the number of drivers making catering deliveries."

These decisions may be pennywise but are often pound-foolish. Entire customer bases may suffer the consequences. Over time, these consumers begin to look elsewhere.

As an independent operator, one of your definitive competitive advantages is the ability to feel and react to your own pulse. Because you are not constrained by the rigidity of large corporate environments, you can be more in tune with your customers' needs. This lets you quickly address issues and fix problems. Inevitably, the value of individual clients will be greater for David than for Goliath. This cumulative impact, over time, can be substantial.

Root For the Home Team

The independent businesses in your area are rooting for you to succeed, as they reflect well on the whole community. Consider this: You decide to landscape your front yard. Soon after, your next-door neighbor does the same, followed by the house across the street. Over time, the whole block follows suit. Eventually, the entire neighborhood is more attractive, demand increases, and home values spike.

A strong independent business community won't drive Goliath away. In fact, it may attract their swagger to the area. Embrace this, because if daily foot traffic increases, your location becomes more desirable and valuable.

Time magazine reports, "When consumers buy from local businesses, twice as much money stays in the community, which means those purchases are twice as efficient in terms of keeping the local economy alive." Furthermore, an increasing number of consumers are embracing the buy local mantra because "there is a profound economic impact on how those dollars affect the communities around the nation and the world."

That is powerful information. Remind your customers that you are a local business.

Looks Can Be Deceiving

Panera describes its product line for catering as "baked goods, salads, sandwiches, soups, beverages." This is actually a somewhat limited menu. It doesn't offer hot entrées or hors d'oeuvres—both significant product lines for corporate catering.

Chipotle offers fajitas and burritos for pickup/catering. This is a very specific menu.

They don't offer breakfast, sandwiches, or a hot entrée variety.

Find a Niche within Your Niche

Goliaths often spend their advertising dollars on mass markets, thereby paying less attention to the smaller niches. By using targeted marketing as a strategy, you can fill the needs of specific industries that desire more menu variety and diversity, including dietary, and allergy-sensitive items.

Connect with Your Clients

Ask questions. Why do people order catering from one of the chains? Suppose they respond, "I know they'll always be here on time."

Try this dialogue:

"It sounds like on-time delivery is your number one priority?"

"Yeah, I guess it is."

"Great. How would you rate their food?"

"It's fine."

"If a caterer was able to provide on-time delivery and food that you would rate as better than 'fine,' perhaps 'really good' or 'great,' would you consider ordering from them?"

"Absolutely."

"Perfect. We are that option."

Bring Your Unique Value to the Marketplace

We tend to underestimate our value as independent operators. When you're making a business transaction, who would you rather deal with, the owner or manager of a local establishment (David) or a disconnected, massive call center (Goliath)?

Your inclination may be, "We need to emulate their slick and shiny packaging or their bestselling menu item." But you don't. You don't need to expend energy and resources in an attempt to mimic your competitor's business model. Instead, focus on what you do better and what makes you unique. There's a reason that customers and clients order from you every day. If they didn't, you wouldn't be in business. Embrace who you are and the brand you have created. David will be proud.

P.S. Go Patriots!

"One of the most important, and most difficult, parts of my job is to strike the delicate balance between being too assertive and not assertive enough."

"I'M NOT A SANDWICH CATERER" . . . *THINK AGAIN.*

Do you ponder whether a drop-off division would affect how your brand is perceived? Have you ever thought *I'm not a sandwich caterer?*

Guess what? It's time to think again. Not only do industry analysts agree that demand in this segment is on the rise and poised for continued growth, but they concur that it is still an under-tapped segment of the industry.

This is good news.

It means a lot of business is waiting to be captured.

Consider this scenario. Elizabeth decides to go into business as Elizabeth the Famous Egg Caterer. She delivers complete breakfasts that featured a choice from six egg dishes:

Omelet, Benedict, Florentine, Frittata, Poached, and Egg & Cheese on Croissants.

Here's the rub. The corporate market has literally *millions* of consumers interested in her services, but they want their eggs either *scrambled* or *hard-boiled.* However, Elizabeth the Famous Egg Caterer doesn't offer these styles.

Why?

Maybe she feels they are not sophisticated enough? For whose tastes (or ego)? Her own? She is not maximizing her businesses potential, and she is leaving money on the table for her competitors.

The real question should be: *Why not?*

She has an operating facility that is licensed, equipped, and staffed. Some significant expenses (e.g., rent and insurance) are fixed costs. She is located within the proximity of a business district and suburban office park. Why not give the people what they want?

Does your full-service catering menu or restaurant offer chicken and beef and salmon? Have you ever considered that these foods can create gourmet sandwiches, such as parmesan-crusted chicken breast on an artisan roll? Or marinated beef with creamy horseradish sauce rollup? How about teriyaki salmon filets as the centerpiece of an entrée lunch salad?

Keep an open mind and think out of the box. The same standards of excellence that are trademarks of your full-service division can just as easily apply to a corporate drop-off division. To keep consistent with your brand, provide upscale paper products and serving ware, and *you are on your way to a new revenue stream.*

The Golden Goose

Plenty of companies that regularly order catering have deep pockets and will pay more for a quality product. Alternatively, if your style is more casual - standard no-frills sandwiches and salads at lower prices are always in demand. Whichever the case, each division can profit from the other. If you have a restaurant/retail operation, cross-promotion adds another layer of branding and growth opportunity.

So, let's say a full-service caterer asks, "Will offering corporate drop-off services affect my brand?" The answer is a resounding "Yes!" Expanding your scope of services and filling a need in the marketplace will *enhance* your brand. *It will make your brand stronger.*

There is no greater testimonial or positive word-of-mouth advertising than a client saying, "I use Elizabeth's Catering for everything. Last spring, they catered my daughter's wedding; last month, it was a surprise party for my husband. And they deliver box lunches to my office twice a week."

The number one reason that more full-service caterers, restaurateurs, grocery stores, and even food truck operators are entering this market segment is the golden goose of corporate drop-off catering—**repeat business.**

The Call of Repeat Business

"We need 50 deluxe box lunches ($15 per person) delivered Monday through Friday next week at 11:45 a.m. and beverages, coffee, and afternoon snacks, such as cheese and crackers or veggie crudité ($7 per person), delivered at 3 p.m."

<u>Let's Do the Math</u>

($15 + $7 = $22)

($22 x 50 people x 5 days = $5,500)

Not a bad jumpstart going into a new week, right?

(P.S. Almost half of our $2 million per year corporate business in Boston is through repeat clients.)

Does your full-service catering business take a noticeable dip in January and February and/or

July and August? The corporate sector is steadier with less fluctuation. This is not theory. It is fact. If you commit to starting or growing a drop-off division, you'll be amazed how those traditionally slower months will get busier.

With a plan, you can create a foundation and a new customer base within six months. Within a year, you will be asking yourself, "What took me so long to get on this train?" If you have an existing base and aspire to take it to the next level, measurable growth can happen even sooner. There are tried-and-true systems to make both scenarios a reality.

The forecast for the corporate catering sector is very encouraging. Now is an ideal time to get in the game. Demand in this multibillion dollar sector is strong and growing. If you are looking for ways to boost your bottom line, generate a new revenue stream, *and* enhance your brand, corporate drop-off catering is your ticket

PUT IT IN WRITING

Like clockwork, it happens every year.

You go to your gym the first week of a new year, and you swear you've walked into the wrong place. *Where did all these people come from?* Usually, by about the middle of the month, things have returned to normal. New Year's resolutions last an average of three weeks.

Studies show that only 10% of us commit our resolutions to paper. Yet, eight in ten people who document their resolutions stick with them all year. There is strong evidence suggesting that when we put our goals in writing, we have a much greater likelihood of success.

A compilation of research studies conducted by sources including the *Harvard Business Review, Forbes Magazine,* and *The New York Times* reveals:

- *About 4% of business owners attain "considerable wealth" during their careers.*

- *About 4% of business owners have written goals.*

Think there's a connection? Day dreaming about our goals is easy—easy to blow off, that is.

As a catering consultant, hearing a client say "I want to create an operations manual for my business" is the equivalent of a personal trainer hearing a client say "I want to lose 20 pounds."

Both are common battle cries.

Both have enormous upsides.

In the vast majority (about 96%) of cases, both are never realized.

I was almost a decade into my career before I began documenting my business goals. However, when I did start this practice, I realized immediate progress.

I began taking action on the ideas that had been marinating in my mind for years. Coincidentally, creating an operations manual for my catering business was at the top of my goals list.

I committed to paper some of the core business theories I practiced and others that I wanted to implement. While these practices can benefit a cross-section of business models, I think they are particularity integral to a successful corporate catering business.

Systems

Systems and processes are the building blocks of a successful business. Every facet of an operation is part of a system that can be managed or improved by applying correct principles. A systems approach to building a successful business eliminates employee indiscretion and replaces it with detailed procedures, standards, and accountability, as well as a method for measuring results. Michael Gerber, author of *E-Myth*, says it best,

"Let systems run the business and people run the systems."

Documentation

Systems documentation—putting everything in writing—is a detailed, thorough strategy for all key routines, daily tasks, and backup plans that are part of a business. The step-by-step information should be organized in a three-ring binder and be accessible and understandable to all employees.

Consistency

Consistency is giving customers what they want—every single time. Repeat business is the golden goose of corporate catering. Creating a successful brand means positively affecting what customers think and how they feel when they hear the company name. I cannot stress enough the importance of Consistency with both your food and your service.

Next, I tackled the standard operating procedure (SOP) for our most commonly sold item, the assorted sandwich platter. As this excerpt from my book *Lessons Learned from our Mistakes* explains, this was a long overdue problem area that needed attention.

Situation

Defining "assorted" sandwiches (customers often ordered "20 assorted sandwiches")

What We Thought Then

Assorted means *assorted*. The sandwich maker will produce an appropriate variety.

What We Know Now

If Carl Carnivore is the sandwich maker, "20 assorted" might include two vegetarian sandwiches (too few). If Valerie Vegetarian is the sandwich maker, "20 assorted" might include 10 vegetarian sandwiches (too many).

Lesson Learned

Consider "assorted" a recipe term that requires definition and documentation. The assortment should be consistent regardless of who the sandwich maker is.

Below is the formula (specs) that we decided on for "Assorted Sandwiches for (20)":

(4) Turkey (20%)

(4) Chicken Salad (20%)

(4) Vegetarian (20%)

(3) Tuna Salad (15%)

(3) Roast Beef (15%)

(2) Ham (10%)

And there we had it. Done! "Assorted" was defined. We finally had a system to ensure the bestselling item on our menu would be consistent. I wondered why we waited so long.

Thus, we began a committed process of putting everything, starting with our goals, in writing. Over time, the SOPs matured into blueprints for running all areas of the business, including food, employee, operational, and administrative policies and procedures.

Over the years, a detailed, thorough, and regularly updated operations manual has increased our bottom-line profit margin by, incredibly, 4%—identical to the percentage of business owners who have put their goals in writing and attained considerable wealth during their careers.

Remember, commitment means doing what you said you were going to do, long after the mood you said it in has left you.

"I strive to be confident enough to prove that I am in charge, but humble enough to admit when I am wrong."

THE MOST IMPORTANT CUSTOMER

I was attending a workshop titled "Sales, Service, and Survival in the Catering Industry."

The keynote speaker, a catering titan, roared from the podium, "If you ever, and I mean *ever*, make a customer feel like they are interrupting your day, I guarantee that within three years, probably sooner, you will be out of business."

He continued, "To realize success in this industry, and I'm not talking about paying your bills and getting by, I'm talking about creating a very comfortable lifestyle, you must make every customer feel they are your most important customer of the day. It is your job to make them feel special." He went on to cite some industry statistics.

Customers are willing to pay more in exchange for better service.

- 75% of customers who switch to a competitor do so because of poor service.

- 95% of unhappy customers will do business with you again if you resolve their issue immediately.

Perhaps most eye opening:

- Only 10% of customers will tell you about a problem or issue they are having with your company. The most common form of expression is to stop doing business with you.

I had an epiphany that day. I (and my staff) would no longer operate under the assumption, "We haven't heard anything to the contrary, so everything must be going well." I began scheduling "check-in" meetings and phone calls with our customers and corporate clients.

THE 10 COMMANDMENTS OF CUSTOMER SERVICE

1) Lead by example.
You need to set the bar. Employees will take their cues from the people they work for. Never complain or speak poorly about a customer in front of your staff because it gives them a license to do the same.

2) Answer the phone and emails.
When the phone rings, answer it—always. Whether it's before you open, after you close, or on a holiday, answer that phone. The call is often a gateway to business for your company.

If a potential customer calls at 10:00 p.m. asking for a proposal, politely explain that you are closed for the day and that someone will get back to them in the morning. This might prevent them from contacting a competitor. (P.S. Make sure someone follows up in the morning.)

Try to return all emails, especially those requesting information the same day. Establish a 24-hour maximum policy to respond to all others.

3) Don't make promises you can't keep.
If you say "I'll email a proposal by 4:00 p.m. tomorrow," do it. If you need more time (which happens), let your customer know before 4:00 p.m.

Suggestion: "Hi, Sara, we're putting together a very thorough proposal
for you, and it's taking longer than we anticipated. Would it be OK if we send it by 10:00 a.m. tomorrow?"

4) Listen actively.
Active listening is the art of rephrasing the key point(s) of what your customer has said, but in the form of a question.

For example: "If I'm understanding correctly, you're on a very tight schedule, and most importantly, all five lunches need to be set up in each conference room absolutely no later than 12:30. Is that correct?"

5) Fix the problem first.
Regardless of where a problem occurred or who was involved, your immediate focus should be resolution.

Suggestion: "Sara, first thing, let's get you 20 more box lunches as quickly as possible. I'll call you later, and we can figure out what happened to cause this miscommunication."

6) Acknowledge mistakes.
Most people respect those who admit mistakes with no excuses attached.

Suggestion: "I apologize that we came up short today, and I understand why you are frustrated. I assure you we will take the necessary steps to ensure this never happens again."

7) Go the extra mile.

Going above and beyond the call of duty means doing something that is not required as part of your professional obligation. It is doing something special or extra. Customers, even challenging ones, often show extreme loyalty when you demonstrate they are important enough to go beyond what is required. They may not always express it, but it usually makes a big impact.

8) Have a professional staff.

If you have thorough job descriptions and a rigorous training program, exceptional customer service skills are very teachable. Your entire staff should be empowered to actively address problems that a customer might encounter.

9) Promote familiarity.

Your delivery staff is often the face of your corporate drop-off business. Have the same employees deliver to the same companies as much as possible. This is a great way to build rapport and business relationships.

10) Remember names.

Customers tend to like you more and assume you are more competent when you use their name a few times during conversations. It makes them feel that you are listening and that you genuinely care.

"Outstanding leaders go out of their way to boost the self-esteem of their personnel. If people believe in themselves, it's amazing what they can accomplish"

WHEN THINGS GO WRONG

When you are on the phone with an upset customer, wait until your customer is finished speaking before you respond. Do not interrupt. Do not try to defend your position. (There may be a time to do so, but now is not it.)

Try this:

Apologize: "I am sorry this happened." (Yes, even if it is not your fault.) "Thank you for bringing it to my attention."

Repeat the issue: "I understand you are regularly running out of napkins during the lunches we are catering for your clients."

Validate: "I appreciate how frustrating this must be for you."

Suggest resolution: "What if we were to drop off a case of backup napkins for you to keep in a storage closet? If you run short again, you will immediate access to more."

Act quickly: Deliver the napkins within 24 hours.

When the dust settles:
Follow up with the customer, preferably by phone. Depending on the circumstances, consider visiting them in person (being armed

with a peace offering of desserts or cheese and crackers never hurts!).

WHAT'S MY JOB?

While a lot of my knowledge has been gleaned from my personal catering experience, I continually learn more as I speak to my clients. Recently, I had a long conversation with one who pointedly said, "Michael, I don't really know what my job is anymore. Am I a catering salesperson, head of marketing, purchasing agent, chef, human resources director, or merely the person who puts out all the daily fires? When I go into work, sometimes I don't know which hat to wear. What is the most important thing I should do?"

A Good Problem to Have

If you have thought about this, it follows that your business is growing. If your business is struggling, you do whatever is necessary to keep the doors open. Maybe you can't afford a full staff, so one day you need to be the driver and another day you may be the dishwasher.

When you start to make money, however, you will find you can afford an extra lunch driver and another part-time cook. As your business grows, every position may be filled with a qualified person, and that leaves you time to work on bigger picture projects. This is the theory of working *on* your business rather than *in* your business.

Reluctant to Delegate?

One of my clients wanted to add breakfast to her catering services, but didn't want to get up at 4:00 am. Instead, she thoroughly trained her staff how to successfully run this part of the operation. Guess what happened? The orders got out, and customers were happy.

However, when it came to lunch, she did not know whether her staff would be able to handle the volume without direct supervision. My advice was that if her crew could learn to execute breakfast successfully, they could be trained to do the same for lunch. I suggested taking advantage of slower business hours and using the time to nurture her employees to grow into new responsibilities—they might pleasantly surprise her. In this case, my client is now opening her fourth location!

Can't Let Go?

This can be a critical point for your operation. If you can take a step back and assign some management responsibility to others, it will allow your business to organically grow, and you can assume a bigger vision role. Those who learn to trust and ultimately delegate to others are often times amazed how their business expands.

Still There

One client tried to run his business from another state. Unfortunately, he couldn't resist the urge to call three or four times a day just to "make sure everything was going OK." His staff became resentful, and this client eventually sold his business. His company had grossed a little more than a million dollars per year when he sold it, and three years later, it generated only half that amount.

During those three years, my client had little or no contact with his former staff. The new owner was a semi-absentee gentleman and made many poor decisions. Still, throughout messy supplier changes, staff turnover, ill-fated menu reworking, and generally poor management, half of the original clients remained three years later.

My client still wonders what he could have accomplished if he had kept the business, enabled and encouraged his staff, and consulted with them on a weekly basis rather than three or four times a day. Although it may have felt right at the time, he realized that micromanaging, especially from afar, was not in the best interest of his business.

SHOULD I STAY OR SHOULD I GO?

In the early years, we did everything. We cooked, cleaned, answered the phones, took orders, placed orders, and delivered orders. When the day was over, it was time to move on to the avalanche of paperwork. As our business grew, we were able to hire employees and delegate some responsibilities.

Today, you are probably somewhere along a delegation continuum that either keeps you very busy with the daily needs of your business, or you have managed to sufficiently train your staff, so you can actually remove yourself from your operation for a day or two (hopefully longer).

I Can't Leave

It's hard to let go. Recently, a client had one of those days when deliveries were late, the wrong food went to the wrong companies, their produce vendor was missing half the order, a van broke down in between deliveries, and one of her biggest accounts was very unhappy because they ran out of food.

She called me, exasperated, asking, "If these things happen when I am here, who knows what disasters will occur if I'm gone? There is no way I can leave my business for an hour, much less a day."

You'll Stay Where You Are

Do *not* take this position. As enlightened owners and managers, we need to give our employees the room to make mistakes and subsequently find ways to correct them. If we can't learn to do that, we will eventually stop our businesses from growing.

Lifelong Learning

We also need to recharge our collective vision and learn to see things from a different perspective. Think about when you return from a vacation, isn't it interesting how things seem slower and more relaxed the day you get back to work?

One of the benefits of getting older, and hopefully wiser, is the ability to look at situations with a more experienced set of eyes. For the first 10 years of my career, I operated under the notion that to maximize my shot at success, I needed to work as hard as I could and put in as many hours as possible. And I think there is some merit to this concept, especially in the early years.

Over time, my perspective has evolved. And I

am grateful it has. I *strongly support* getting away from the business every year. Removing yourself away from the day-to-day routine to enjoy different scenery and new experiences and to recharge the batteries is good for the mind and the soul. And don't underestimate the break it gives your employees from you and, perhaps, the appreciation it engenders as well.

(P.S. If you are thinking to yourself *I can't remember the last time I took a vacation,* please call me; we need to talk).

"The greatest leaders are those who remain calm and decisive in the face of a crisis."

A PLAYBOOK FOR YOUR BUSINESS

Someone in your organization should be able to successfully run things while you are gone. This is an important reason to develop an operations manual for your business. Creating a step-by-step playbook detailing how all s of your operation are run is the key to producing a consistent product and controlling costs.

Where to Begin?

You can start by documenting the exact description of a sandwich.

For example

- How many ounces of meat?
- How many slices/ounces of cheese?
- What type of lettuce?
- How many tomato slices?
- Are condiments on the bread or do they come on the side?
- How is the sandwich constructed?
- Is it sliced sideways or diagonally?
- Is there a labeling system?

- Do you use toothpicks?

Let's say you have a standing order every week to deliver 20 sandwich box lunches to Shark & Shark Attorneys. With an operations manual, whoever is making the sandwiches has set guidelines to follow. Every client will receive the same consistent, high-quality sandwich week in and week out.

Accompanying each sandwich is one pickle, two packets of mayonnaise, two packets of mustard, one chocolate chip cookie, one bottle of spring water, one plastic plate, and two napkins. The written description of how this sandwich box lunch is made and packaged is *not* a guideline, and it is not up to the discretion of the employee. *It is the Bible.*

You should have written recipes for all the food you prepare. Regardless of who makes the tuna salad, the chicken soup, or the marinated flank steak, the product should look, taste, and be presented the same every time it is delivered to a customer.

If you don't have an operations manual, you are in the majority. But think about a target date to start one. Success begins with preparation and a game plan. Your goal is to create a step-by-step roadmap for running your business Remember that it is a living document, meaning you will always be working on it to some extent as you come up with new menu ideas or refine the way you do things.

SAME-DAY ORDERS . . . WHAT TO DO?

Full-service caterers generally have sufficient notice to plan for their events, although last-minute requests for catering for funerals and even for weddings (though not very often), occur.

When you enter the realm of drop-off catering, however, the rules drastically change. Breakfasts, lunches, and dinners for any number of guests can and will be requested, sometimes with only an hour or two notice.

If you've got 10 orders for lunch, and they're all choreographed perfectly so that the food arrives on time, a last-minute order can be a challenge.

Note that I did not characterize the last-minute order as a "problem." I call it a challenge for a reason because there are numerous ways to handle these situations and capture more business. But you need to take that last-minute order.

Why?

√ If the order is from an active customer, he or she naturally depends on you to provide the service. If you can't, there will be someone else out there who can.

√ Maybe the order is indeed from a customer who has had an order denied by their regular caterer. In this case, you can start a long-term relationship by solving the customer's problem.

√ Maybe a last minute meeting was called, and the team leader needs food delivered ASAP. For whatever reason, someone found your number or pulled up your website. Service this new customer properly, and you might begin a long-term relationship.

√ Possibly, a regular customer simply forgot to order. They'll look really bad if their lunch doesn't arrive. If you can save them, it strengthens the relationship in spades.

√ It is important that your entire staff, from the head chef to the delivery drivers, is on board with this concept. They are a regular piece of your business.

√ A new customer misunderstood the ordering process. Maybe they're used to merely calling a restaurant an hour before they need their food. You can explain your ordering guidelines later. But for now, take the order.

Remember, your regular clients and potential customers most likely do not understand the inner workings of your business, and they shouldn't be expected to do so. They don't care how many orders you have, or that two employees have called in sick, or a delivery vehicle just broke down. You advertise that you deliver great food on time, and people will call you for that reason.

In summary, when a client asks me, "What do I do about those pain-in-the-butt last-minute orders?" I say, **"Take them."**

The next question is usually, "What am I supposed to do when a customer calls at 9:30 a.m. asking for 50 box lunches at noon, and we are already maxed out for deliveries?"

Try this:

"We would be happy to accommodate your order. "We're booked solid for noon but could deliver to you by 12:30. Would that work for you?"

The next question is usually, "What if they say that 12:30 doesn't work and they need it by noon?"

Try this:

"I realize this isn't as convenient, but is it possible that someone from your company could come to our location and pick the order up? We will move your order ahead in the production cue, so we can have ready for you by 11:30."

The next question is usually, "What if they say they don't have anyone who can pick it up?"

Try this:

"We work with a courier service or (cab company or Uber) that will deliver your order by noon. There will be some additional delivery costs, but we will handle that and add it to your invoice."

Suggestion:

You and your staff should avoid using the word *no*. Instead, tell the customer what you *can* do for them.

Fact:

You can print, say, yell, or post, "We require 24 hours notice for catering orders" until the cows come home. The reality is, handling same-day orders are a part being a successful corporate caterer. In fact, as your business grows, demand for these orders will increase.

Tip:

In the policies section of your menu, include the following:

24-hours notice is requested for all orders. For larger groups and specialty items, a 48-hour may be required. However, we have created a smaller "short-notice menu" (i.e., *production friendly*) and will always accommodate same-day orders to the best of our abilities.

Fact:

A solid 10% (15% in some years) of our almost $2-million a-year corporate catering business in Boston is same-day orders. In fact, it would be unusual not to receive at least a couple every day.

Embrace them:

A successful drop-off catering day requires serious planning. By Tuesday afternoon at 5:00, for example, you and your staff should have a game plan to handle Wednesday's business. Whatever systems you have in place should be helping to ensure that Wednesday's orders are produced to your specifications and delivered on time.

But what do you do on Wednesday when two customers request food at the last minute? Your kitchen staff should be able to produce a couple more orders, but how do you get them delivered on time?

Creative solutions for dealing with unexpected orders:

√ Give yourself some time flexibility to double-up deliveries. Your telephone answerer should be trained to ascertain the last-minute customer's actual eating time. Even if the customer requests an 11:30 delivery, he or she may not really need the food on the premises until 11:50 for it to be served at noon. This way, a driver with an 11:30 delivery could also take the new 11:50 order.

Going further, you could call the original 11:30 delivery and ask them if it would be OK to arrive just 10 minutes earlier. This gives your driver even more time. Most existing customers will agree to this if you don't request this accommodation too often.

√ Carefully analyze the day's orders. If you have a simple box lunch order for 10 people scheduled to be delivered at 11:30 and you'd like to deliver it earlier - call and ask if the office has a refrigerator large enough to store their lunches.

√ If your customer gives the OK, deliver that order ASAP, even if it's only 9:30. In actuality, it doesn't make much difference if the already prepared box lunches sit in your refrigerator or your customer's. Now you have a driver available for the new order.

√ Every employee is a potential driver. Team up with them to get the job done. If your dishwasher does not speak English, for example, and your office manager is not able to lift heavy boxes, you may have a match made in catering heaven. Have the office manager drive the dishwasher to the location. The manager can properly communicate with the customer, while the dishwasher can haul in and set up the order.

√ Call Aunt Rose and Uncle Bob. Obviously, not all drop-off orders are suitable for "amateur delivery," but many are. If your relatives are available, they may be happy to help you out on a busy day. If you've really planned ahead, you will have previously "trained" Rose and Bob in the rudimentary skills of drop-off delivery, and they'll be ready to go.

√ Call those who make money from your business. The print shop across the street that produces your menus, the restaurant next door where you fill your sushi orders, the service station where your delivery vehicles are repaired, and especially your vendor reps—all of these businesses have potential drivers. Never say never. We have gotten through our share of difficult delivery days because took a chance and made a phone call.

√ Train a local courier service to take your orders. One Midwest client often used a messenger service to deliver catering orders on time. They started with simple box lunch and cold food orders. After six months, the messenger service was setting up hot buffets.

"My employees don't have to like me. But they must respect me."

MAKE SURE YOUR CLIENTS KNOW THE DIFFERENCE

Recently, I read an article about an app-less food delivery service; all steps of the process—from ordering to delivery—are handled by text. Almost every week, I see new middlemen emerging who make it very easy for anyone to order any kind of food from anywhere.

If you own a restaurant, this can be great news for you. However, there are caveats and issues. Most restaurant owners will welcome these services. Caterers, however, may need to pay attention.

Started Small

Many of us built our businesses on small orders. In the beginning, if a potential customer asked if we would deliver three box lunches, we were usually more than happy to oblige. As we grow, these orders can present a dilemma—whether they come from repeat customers or new ones.

Legendary Mike Roman's answer to the regular customer who wanted to know the cost of a three box lunch delivery was, "Mrs. Smith, if you really need only three box lunches I will produce and deliver them for free, since there is no way for me to make a profit on such a small order. When I add your order into the billing process I actually lose money; I value you as a customer, and that's more important than the few pennies I will make or lose on this order, so what time do you need the food delivered?"

One Problem

One obvious problem is that today, Mrs. Smith can contact a number of services that will welcome her three-meal business, and maybe we should let her. If she really wants three restaurant meals dropped off at her desk in brown paper bags after they have travelled on the floor or in the back seat of some unknown driver's random vehicle, then maybe it's time to stop worrying about it. What we do need to do, however, is find a way to communicate that what we do is more than mere food delivery. Because as caterers, we do a lot of things:

- Consult with clients about menu choices.
- Advise them on proper food quantities.
- Prepare food in a controlled environment within a licensed facility.
- Employ professional drivers.
- Inspect and clean our delivery vehicles.

- Ensure proper food temperature at all times.
- Pay our employees a living wage.

Can Favor, Seamless, DoorDash, Foodler, Uber, and the rest claim the same? How are they going to handle a 50-person delivery? Do these middlemen really care if the food is late? Have any of these drivers passed a ServSafe course?

We're Different

As caterers, we need to remind our customers and potential customers that we are indeed in business to **cater** to them as we, as Google defines it, "provide them with food and drink in a professional capacity." We look at the big picture, and that entails more than merely delivering a brown bag of food.

THIRD-PARTY DELIVERY SERVICE: THREAT OR OPPORTUNITY?

If you've trained your staff to deliver properly, you can train the staff at a courier service to do the same thing. If the courier company senses a load of repeat business, you will find a delivery partner who will be willing and able to respond quickly to your needs.

This brings us to UberEATS, Seamless, Grub Hub, EZ Cater, and others that we label as middlemen or third-party delivery services. Some of these may act as pure alternative delivery services for those individuals looking for a sandwich from their favorite restaurant, and others present themselves as a varied menu-intense portal where an office manager can easily order a meal for a small meeting or a large presentation.

Of course, these services come with a price. While charges vary, both the customer and you as the caterer may have to pay. In fact, it is common for these services to bill caterers 10%–15% to deliver your order.

My clients are concerned about all the implications these services present, and they ask me questions like this daily:

- "Should I be using one of these services?"

- "What about the commission they take?"

- "Are some companies better than others?"

- "Are the commissions negotiable?"

- "Can I adjust my catering menu prices when using them to offset some of the commission they receive?"

- "Can I add more delivery fees to "those" orders to offset some commission?"

- "What happens when I am doing business with a company and then suddenly they tell me that they now need to order through Seamless or whomever?"

- "It seems like some of the third-party portals allow me to adjust our prices and others don't?"

Buyer Beware

1. If you use a third-party delivery service, you lose control of your food. If it's your delivery staff, you know which driver is best for every delivery situation. Paul may be good at the grunt work of hauling in large orders, but Janice is better with finicky customers.

The following scary quote is from an Uber driver:

> "I have done the food delivery stuff, and there are usually problems. I was hired to deliver people to places – not food. Uber is just going too fast. They should keep doing what they have proved they can do— legitimate gypsy cab business. I will not walk up several flights of stairs to deliver some lazy ass a meal and listen to his complaints about not getting the sauce he wanted. "F" that."

Do you want that guy delivering your food?

2. The 10%–15% delivery charge that **you** incur can add up to an appreciable sum and will obviously increase your food cost.

3. Some of these companies put all the blame for mistakes directly on you. Check out the Seamless FAQs found on their website:

Who should I call if there is a problem with my order?

The restaurant is the best initial contact for order inquiries. If your order is late or the restaurant made a mistake in fulfilling your order, please contact them directly.

My food arrived and there is something wrong with my order.

It is most efficient for you to contact the restaurant directly so they can quickly offer you a resolve your problem.

Where is my food?

It is most efficient for you to contact the restaurant regarding the status of your order.

I received a confirmation estimating my time of delivery and now the order is late.

Seamless electronically conveys your order to the restaurant. To check on the status of your order, please contact the restaurant directly.

The bottom line is that once Seamless has the order, you are left to handle any problems and clean up the mess they may have caused.

The reality is that some form of third-party delivery is here to stay, and it probably makes sense to get with the program in such a way that benefits you while minimizing possible risk, exposure, and damage to your reputation.

So how do you do that?

If you do lots of business with these services, this is a **way outside-the-box suggestion.** Consider creating a new company division. Give it a new name, a different phone number, unique domain, and a menu tailored to fit the parameters of the third-party delivers. When setting prices, build in a 15% commission. That takes care of any wasted time negotiating commissions with any of the providers. If they deliver your order late, your regular customers will never know it was you.

If a regular customer suddenly tells you that they now have to order through Seamless only, you can send them to your new division. There may also be some interesting added benefits. You may be surprised when your new business competes directly with your existing company, and you will probably insight into the way your clients put catering services out for bid.

This concept is not new, as plumbers, electricians, and pest control services have been using it for years. And while it will take some work to set up properly, this method will stop any agonizing about these third-party services. You can keep your existing catering business pure and separate, and at the same time, you can totally embrace this new technology. That actually may be the best of both worlds.

* We are not offering legal advice, so check with your lawyers and accountants, but in most states, this is as easy as filing a DBA application that allows you to use your existing entity structure along with all of your existing financial accounts.

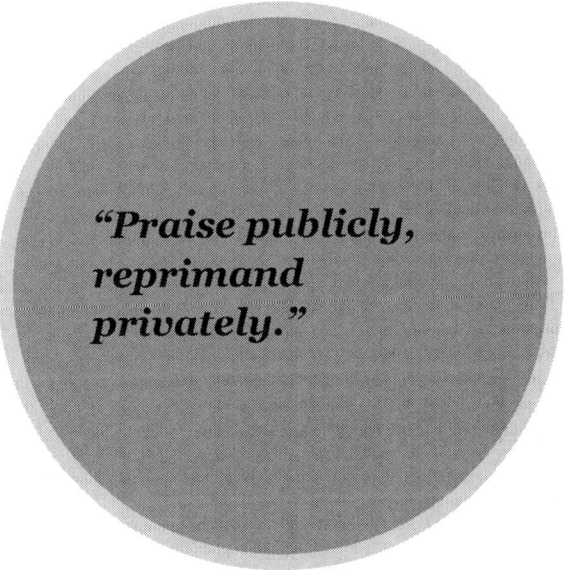

"Praise publicly, reprimand privately."

GETTING ORGANIZED: FILING YOUR WAY TO PROFITABILITY

Setting up an efficient filing system may not be glamorous; however, if done properly, it will absolutely help your bottom line. A user-friendly filing system will make the work day more efficient for you and for any employees who are permitted access to checklists, worksheets, and order forms as part of their job responsibilities.

If you don't have any filing cabinets, get some. If you have a filing system in place, take a close look at how you have it set up. Have at least one separate drawer for

VENDORS
 CUSTOMERS
EMPLOYEES
FINANCIALS
MARKETING

Get cabinets that have at least one more drawer than you think you will need. You will need the space. Keep a separate filing area for your personal life.

Next, get plenty of hanging files, manila/polypropylene folders, and a label maker. Heavy-duty polypropylene folders will not tear and are water repellent. They will cost a little more but last forever.

Then decide on a system of categorization and labeling. If you are not sure how to begin, create "major categories" such as

Bank Statements
Produce Invoices
Workers Compensation

A pattern will emerge. Then you can further subcategorize these topics. You may take

<u>Bank Statements</u> and break it down into

Checking Account
Savings Account
Commercial Loan

The more specific you label your files and folders now, the better your system will work in the future. For example, instead of having one big file for beverage vendors, break it down into several folders, such as

Coca-Cola
Snapple
Poland Spring

The same is true for your overhead expenses. Have separate files for

Telephone
Gas
Electric

Set up action files, such as

Articles to Read
Topics for Next Staff Meeting
Office Supplies Needed

Consider your filing cabinets as a constant work in progress. Create new categories when necessary. A good rule of thumb is if something comes across your desk and you can't quickly determine where to file it, you probably need a new folder.

Regarding the infamous **MISCELLANEOUS** file, ditch it! Why? Because inevitably, this folder will be six inches thick and will lead you back to the black hole of inefficiency.

Two more tips on filing: First, train yourself and your staff to put new documents in the *front* of each folder, *not the back*. This way, the most recent information is the most accessible.

Second, set a day at the end of the calendar or fiscal year and purge your files. Throw out what you do not need, put required records into storage, and keep only what is absolutely necessary in your active files. You will probably be able to purge at least 50% of your paperwork. Always check with your accountant about how long to retain financial records.

Your corporate catering operation is a business, and you need to operate it as such. Establishing a great filing system may not be as enjoyable as developing new menu items or nabbing a big corporate account, but it is important for long-term success. It also allows your operation to run smoothly when you're not there. Having the information is important; being able to find it is even more important. By creating a solid filing structure and exercising the discipline to utilize it consistently, you are taking another step towards streamlining your workflow.

ORGANIZED CHAOS

My definition of *organized* is, "being able to find what you need, when you need it." The world of drop-off catering is hectic enough without a sea of papers, orders, mail, and to-do lists cluttering the office.

A good rule of thumb is to try to handle every piece of paper that comes across your desk once. That means making an immediate decision when you pick up something new: act on it, file it, or throw it away. Many items end up in the last category, so making that decision immediately will save a lot of time and clutter.

As you set out to purge your workspace, be aggressive. Throw away or shred all out-of-date material, and ditch the junk mail and catalogs that you are never going to look at. Stack all the unopened mail that has accumulated, and open it. If you pay your bills online, get rid of all the return envelopes and assorted information that comes with bills these days. Separate all of the material you need to have, and sort it into appropriate piles.

In general, you are going to have to pay it, file it, record it, respond to it, sign it, or scan it. Then act on each pile immediately, and do not stop until you have finished with it.

A clean desk really does help create a sense of order. One of the goals as the owner of your business is that you want the company to operate smoothly without being dependent on your presence. This means that if you are meeting with a client, running errands, or caring for your child, it is easy for your staff to find anything they may need. If an employee has to call a vendor for an emergency delivery, it should not be a treasure hunt to find the phone number or to know who to ask for.

Keeping on top of paperwork should be a top priority. If your desk looks like a hazardous waste site, clean it up, and get a handle on it now. Then establish a daily routine that brings some peace of mind to this part of the operation. You will find this leads to more success for your corporate catering business and will place you in a better position to expand your customer base.

EVERY DOLLAR COUNTS

As independent business owners, we are constantly adding up costs. We may look at the number of customers we have, calculate that we serve 10,000 per year, and rationalize that if we could squeeze another dollar per customer we would have $10,000 more at the end of the year. An extra 10 grand sounds good, right? So now we try and figure out how we are going to create that extra dollar.

One way would be to raise prices. But we need to be careful. Perhaps, we increased (I prefer the term "adjusted") our prices a year ago. Maybe we are already the highest priced caterer in the market. So, we begin to look at other ways to find that dollar.

A good area to start is pricing from our vendors. As we started our business, we may have used multiple vendors. Some of us have seen the value of putting our purchasing power to work by concentrating our buying with one or two large sources. Others may be, for various reasons, loyal to numerous smaller vendors. Regardless, we may decide to test the proverbial waters and put our product list out for bid.

If you are organized, this can be done efficiently. Granted, it will require some time and effort. You (or perhaps someone else in your organization) need to contact the companies, schedule meetings, (have them come to you), be direct, and say, "We need more aggressive pricing." (And P.S., "We don't want to see it creeping back up in a couple of months, *and we will be checking*.")

Let's say that you pay $9 per case for soda (or pop or tonic, depending what part of the country you're in) and order 35 cases a week. Get your price to $8.50 a case, and you've saved $875. You're paying $6 per case for spring water and buying 10 cases a week? Tell your rep they need to come down to $5.25, or you'll buy 40 cases once a month from your local food warehouse. You've just saved another $375.

It *does* happen like that. In most cases, all you have to do is ask (just like a regular client asks you if there was a way to shave $.50 per person off their $500 lunch order every Tuesday and Thursday). You usually find a way to make it work, right?

"Leadership is not about titles, positions, or flow charts. It is about one life influencing another."

FIVE TIPS FOR CONTROLLING CATERING COSTS

1) Keep your service vendors competitive.

Let your laundry, chemical, and trash removal companies know that you will put their contracts out to bid once a year—and then do it. These are all competitive industries. Make sure you are not overpaying.

2) Look closely at your food invoices.

Keep a vigilant eye on your invoices. If a price looks askew, call your vendor and ask about it. This will encourage them to sharpen their pencil when market conditions affect pricing. And, it will put them on notice that you are paying attention to their pricing.

In fact, don't just check the invoices—get out the scale. Spot-check weights on chicken, fish, meat, and produce. If you are being charged for 20 pounds of chicken breast and you received 18.5 pounds, a call to your vendor should straighten out any future "weight miscalculations."

3) Shop creatively.

Think outside the box—both in where you shop for food and in what you buy. Check out discount food warehouses, such as Restaurant Depot, where it's possible to save 15%–25% off of wholesale prices. Consider creative uses of lower-cost food items, such as pork and tenderloin butts that are medium-priced entrees at higher-profit margins.

4) Consider leasing appliances.

It can be very difficult to get financing from a bank for restaurant equipment because it is viewed as a higher-risk loan. Also, you can write leasing off 100%, and do not have to factor in depreciation." I would rather invest my liquid cash in other areas of expanding the business.

5) Be mindful of energy costs.

Regarding utilities, many states now have private utility providers, so it pays to shop around for the most aggressive pricing. Taking simple steps, such as switching out traditional light bulbs for more cost-efficient LED bulbs, can result in noticeable cost savings. Furthermore, confirm that any of your leased equipment is as energy efficient as possible.

Finally, make sure your staff is doing all the things your mother told you to do—turn off lights that are not being used, keep all refrigerators and freezers shut, and close the windows when the air conditioner is on.

It is no secret that controlling costs is important in any business, especially in the food service industry, where the profit margins are notoriously thin. In addition to these tips, consider budgeting food costs, determine proper price points, and maintain appropriate inventory levels.

HOW TO SURVIVE A CATERING CASH FLOW CRISIS

All successful business owners know that you need to analyze, understand, and get in front of impending cash flow problems. Never wait until the last minute to act because the day you cannot pay your employees and/or the day Sysco moves your account to COD can be disastrous. You should be savvy enough to know well in advance when cash trouble is lurking.

However, if you wake up one day and acknowledge the reality of a financial crisis, then it is *not* the time for in-depth analyses of what got you where you are. There will be plenty of opportunities for a mea culpa after you have found a way to stay in business. Absolutely, do not dwell on your company's fragile condition; instead, spend all of your energy figuring out how to raise cash.

Following are client-proven methods for creating cash flow:

1) Put off paying bills. You may be surprised that those vendors you previously labeled "unlikely to help" may give you a break.

a) If your $10,000 rent is due on the first of the month, for example, walk into the landlord's office with four post-dated $2,500 checks over the next four weeks. And don't blame yourself for the problem; tell the landlord that business is good, but collections have slowed; all the issues are temporary, and you will be back on track shortly. Chances are that he or she will take your money.

b) Tell every supplier that you have a temporary cash flow issue and need more time to pay. Make personal visits to vendor credit managers and possibly contact someone higher up the management chain. True deadbeats who intend to disappear rarely show up at the credit manager's office. If you are up-front, your candidness and forthrightness will be appreciated.

2) Get new suppliers. If you have caught the situation early and are not behind on your current supplier bills, you may be able to get a few new suppliers with fresh credit lines.

3) Check your receivables, and call in favors. Done carefully, you can use this technique to raise cash without damage to your company's image. When you call the accounts payable person responsible for your account, say, "I need a favor. I am reaching out to my best

paying clients because a number of less-than-perfect payers have left me with a temporary problem. Is there any way you can process our invoices a little sooner this month?"

One of my clients sent me this script, and he maintained that when used judiciously, it got him out of trouble more than once.

4) Offer an immediate discount for COD orders. Send out a mass customer email, and announce that for one week only, you will take "X" percent off all invoices that are paid COD.

5) Have a sale. Sell box lunches for $7.50 instead of $8.50 if the orders are prepaid.

A combination of the above measures should take some of the pressure off during a catering cash flow crisis. If you still are in trouble, you can consider borrowing money from other sources.

"Surround yourself with great people; delegate authority; get out of the way"

HOW TO GET PAID FASTER

Caterers who are used to getting paid the day of the event will have to shift their mindset as they move into the corporate catering realm. Companies often require payment terms of 30 days; in other words, you'll have to wait for your money. And, like any business that extends credit, someone in your organization will always be chasing money. The more business you do, the more receivables and past-due accounts you will have.

To position your company for getting paid on time, consider the following:

• Always discuss payment terms and procedures with new customers as soon as the relationship has begun and absolutely no later than the time the first order is placed.

• Never assume that the person who places the order will be responsible for the actual invoice payment.

• Find out if the company prefers printed or emailed invoices.

• Ask if a purchase order is required. Some companies will issue a check unless your invoice includes a valid purchase order number. If you do need a purchase order number, ask who gives it to you, and get it immediately.

• Ask about W-9 requirements. Many companies cannot issue a check without a completed W-9 from your business.

• There may be a vendor questionnaire that needs to be completed before a check will be cut. You may have to answer questions about the status of your business, for example, whether it is owned by a minority or a woman.

• Inquire about exactly where to send the invoice. Many companies have accounts receivable departments with specific addresses.

• Try to establish a connection with someone in the accounts payable department. With a few magic keystrokes, they may be able to accelerate the payment process.

• Find out if your new customer requires monthly statements in addition to individual invoices. Some will not pay from an individual invoice alone.

• Understand the company's payment terms. Many companies will pay all of September's invoices, for example, at the end of October. Therefore, you could legitimately have to wait 60 days for payment on an early September invoice.

TIP

Set up a system where the actual invoice is delivered with the order. Have two copies. The driver gets it signed and leaves a copy with the client. Print "**This is Your Invoice**" at the top. You still may need to send duplicate copies, but this does help with the companies that pay as they go, as opposed to one check per month.

• Offer a discount for immediate payment. A "2/10" discount offer tells your customer that if they pay within 10 days, you will give them a 2% discount. Think of this like a credit card transaction, where you can easily pay up to a 3.5% commission to the credit card processor.

• Include an electronic payment option on your emailed invoice. If there is a button that allows a customer to remit by PayPal or through Stripe, your customer may take care of your invoice before others that require written checks.

• Invoice promptly. This may seem obvious, but if you are extremely busy at the end of the month and miss a cutoff date, you could wait another 30 days for your cash.

Translating into Dollars

If you do $1 million in catering sales per year, you need to be prepared to have floating receivables that could reach the $100,000 mark. While it may feel great to know that within 30 to 60 days you will have $100,000 in your bank account, this obviously can cause cash-flow issues

WHERE TO FIND CASH IN A PINCH

If you've ever tried to get a bank loan to start a restaurant or catering company and felt that you'd have a better shot of winning the lottery, you are not alone. Restaurants and caterers are generally unloved by standard banking institutions.

About 10 years ago, a novel lending method became available—it's called a merchant cash advance. A great website called Card Payment Options defines this financial tool:

> A merchant cash advance is a financing option that provides merchants with a large up-front sum of cash in exchange for a percentage of future sales. Usually, merchants can qualify for a merchant cash advance simply by providing minimal documentation to prove that they process above a certain amount of credit and debit card sales per month. Merchant cash advance providers then collect a percentage of all future card sales until the original amount plus interest is repaid.

It Works Like This

A merchant cash advance provider looks at your credit card volume. You usually have to submit three months of credit card processing statements and three months of bank statements. The company will check your personal credit score, but it is more concerned with sales volume. Then, based upon their formula, the cash advance provider will offer to advance your business a certain sum. For example, if you run $30,000 of credit card charges per month, the provider may offer to deposit $20,000 in your account. However, the cost of the advance can be steep, as the provider will require that you pay back a much larger amount, probably $26,000 in this case.

This is where the word *advance* is significant, because although not as prevalent today, some states do have laws that ban usurious lending. Since you are technically receiving an advance and not a loan, these laws may not apply.

The provider gets repaid through your daily credit card transactions. Typically, you will have to turn over up to a third of your daily credit card receipts until your advance is paid.

Advantages

- If your business is slow, you pay back less on a daily basis. If you have no credit card transactions for a week, for example, you would pay back nothing.

- Since this is an advance, it does not need to show up as a loan on your balance sheet.

- You don't necessarily "feel it," because you never write a check directly to the processor. (But in reality, you "feel it.")

- The advance term is not fixed; if business is good, you will most likely pay off the advance quicker.

- Credit requirements are more flexible than with standard financing.

- You can set this upwithin a week and get quick cash.

Disadvantages

- This is loan shark money. Usually the terms of these loans are meant to be six months or less. Real interest rates can be exorbitant.

- You need to begin paying the funds back immediately. If you are advanced money on Tuesday, a portion of your Wednesday credit card deposits go directly to the provider.

- Once you start, it may be the beginning of a dangerous cycle. As soon as you have finally paid off your advance, you can get another one. Actually, if you have paid your initial advance down to a few thousand dollars, the provider may offer to roll it into a new deal, thereby increasing the actual interest rate even more.

- Providers may require you to switch credit card processors. In this case, make certain that all of your terms, conditions, and payment percentages do not change.

According to industry expert Steve Nicastro,

> The merchant cash advance industry is not subject to federal regulation, because merchant cash advances are structured as commercial transactions and not loans. Instead, they are regulated by the Uniform Commercial Code in each state, as opposed to banking laws, such as the Truth in Lending Act.

This is a slippery slope. Be very careful. You could get into more debt quickly.

"I cannot give you a formula for success, but I can give you the formula for failure, which is: try to please everybody."

AVOIDING THE TURNOVER TURNSTYLE

I'm not claiming to have a crystal ball, but **this is what I wrote in 2011:**

> Even though we are in the very beginning stages of the economic recovery, and even if your job posts on Craigslist net you 50 or more applicants, **this will not always be the case.** Although this recession was unusually deep and nasty, **unemployment will eventually drop.**
>
> Now is the time to position yourself for the coming changes. If you were in business five years ago, you will remember the **chronic food service labor shortages** that plagued many operators. Whether this occurs again late this year, or next year, now is the time to position yourself to blunt the effects of the inevitable tightness that will occur in the labor market.

My client base gives me a good idea of exactly what is going on in the industry. While slow business trends and rising food costs were even recently the most prevalent complaints, now I hear other gripes:

- My help-wanted posts yield no applicants.
- I can't seem to find anyone to work.
- I have seen a huge employee turnover.
- My workers are increasingly unreliable.
- I am forced to pay higher wages for lower quality employees.
- I can barely get the food out.

I'll always remember when a client from California called me in 2009 and said, "I had to offer $15.00 per hour to an unkempt musician, and I had to beg him to start immediately. He was going to be the paper packer! After two days, he said, 'Sorry, man, I gotta go. Someone else offered me $17.00,' and he was out the door."

Three Strategies to Retain Long-Time Employees

Offer incentives

Carefully crafted incentives for accomplishing tasks from your action plans can keep your staff motivated and attuned to the customers. What if you gave 1% of your gross sales to your employees? Do you think they might be happier on a very busy day?

Give bonuses

One of my clients had an annual contract to provide hot breakfasts within a two-hour window to 50 different school locations. In the afternoon, after everything was successfully delivered and subsequently picked up, the owner handed out $50 bills to all staff members in thanks for their efforts. His employees actually looked forward to this challenging day each year.

Understand issues

Employees have personal issues; they have medical appointments, an important family event and parenting responsibilities. Yes, the orders have to be processed and delivered, but great bosses help their staff members to find time to take care of their personal business. Remember, one of your ownership perks is that you can come and go as you please; your employees can't.

BE TRUE TO YOUR TASTINGS

One of the best vehicles for generating new corporate catering business is offering potential clients a complimentary tasting—a sampling of your food.

Typically, you would make the presentation to the administrators responsible for placing orders.

Your tastings *must* to be true representations of what the actual orders will look and taste like. You do not want to make a stupendous presentation that you cannot live up to it when you start regular service. All this does is set the potential new client up for disappointment.

A lot of work can go into simply arranging for a tasting. The process usually includes persistent prospecting, cold calling, qualifying, scheduling, and confirming.

Yes, you want the food to present well and taste great. *But, don't do anything differently from a typical delivery.* In other words, if your usual sandwich portion size of turkey is 1/3 pound, don't bring 1/2-pound sandwiches to the tasting. If your standard plastic ware is medium weight white, don't bring heavy weight black.

You need to sell your food and services in exact unison with what a customer should expect when they place an order. While you may be tempted to impress a potential new client by pulling out all the stops during a tasting, they won't be clients for long you if their first couple of orders don't live up to the expectations you have created.

THE UNHAPPY CUSTOMER

We all know that our customers pay our bills. Building your business is a process that requires hard work, patience, and persistence. Creating a customer base can be exciting as you see it begin to evolve. You need to keep up that same effort after a customer (who orders consistently) becomes a client (who does most, if not all, of their business with you).

Never, ever, ever take your clients, especially the bigger ones, for granted. Stay in touch with them regularly. Visit them occasionally. Go above and beyond whenever possible, and always remember to thank them for their business.

Every day will not be perfect. Inevitably, problems and misunderstandings will arise with your customers and clients. Some situations will have an obvious resolution, and others will be more challenging. The ability to professionally resolve issues requires forethought and experience.

Three Strategies to Handle an Upset Customer

1) Disengage, which is basically taking a time-out for adults. For example, say a customer is

taking you to task because the sauce for their chicken "was supposed to come on the side." You, as the person who took the order, recollect a very different conversation. Maybe it's the end of what's been a long, difficult day for you both, and you can sense the dialogue is beginning to ramp up.

Ask your customer, "May I put you on hold for a minute? I want to talk to someone in the kitchen and get some more information." This gives you both a chance to calm down, reset, and respond appropriately.

If you need more than a few minutes, try saying, "The catering chef is meeting with another client at the moment; may I call you back within the hour?"

If a good night's sleep will give you both a new perspective, (which nine times out of ten it does), consider saying, "I want to get this resolved to your satisfaction. May I call you tomorrow and we will get this squared away?

2) Defuse the situation. For example, a customer calls at 10:45 a.m. and wants to cancel their order that is scheduled for 11:30 a.m., which is already loaded on a truck and about to leave. When you explain why it's too late, the customer responds, "Well I thought I

had until 11 a.m. to cancel an order."

Instead of responding the way you occasionally might fantasize about ("11 a.m.! Are you out of your mind??!! By 11 a.m., your order is long gone"), gracefully assume some of the responsibility by saying, "Perhaps we could have been more thorough in confirming that you understood the cancellation policy. I am sorry." Or, "Maybe the wording on our menu regarding our cancellation policy needs to be looked at. I apologize if it was not clear."

3) Don't take the bait. Not responding to aggressive or negative statements requires some self-discipline. If you focus on them, you will spend more time debating their merit, as opposed to resolving the issue. Here's an example of a proper way to handle a tough customer:

> **Customer:** "What's *wrong* with your delivery person? I *told* him where to set up the order. Do they not listen? Or do they just do whatever they feel like doing?"

> **Response:** "I understand your frustration that your breakfast was delivered to the wrong room, and I am sorry this happened. Bob is a very good delivery person. I can assure you that it was an honest

miscommunication. I will be happy to send him back to your office right now to move the breakfast to another conference room."

This response allows the aggressive statement, "Do they just not listen?" to pass right over, and you have offered the most immediate solution possible. Once you are able to master this skill, you and your staff will become pros at handling your customers.

"Remember that not getting what you want is sometimes a wonderful stroke of luck."

AULD LANG SYNE

When your last holiday catering order has been successfully executed, I strongly encourage you to enjoy what is left of the holiday season with those you care about. Take a well-deserved break from the emails, phone calls, proposal requests, and the multiple challenges you face daily.

Next, it's time for your year-end catering evaluation. By the first week of the new year, take a look at where your business stands. Did you make a profit? Are you optimistic about next year's prospects? Do you still like what you are doing? This is a great time for a thorough company analysis as you try to put yourself in the best position for success and continued growth.

Following are some things you should consider:

Costs

One of the first things new business owners learn is that everyone wants your money. The minute you get your website up and the doors, open, you are contacted by accountants, lawyers, trash services, laundry services, Internet marketers, linen companies, and many more. Some of these purveyors will win your business, and every month you'll send them money. Now is the time to make sure your costs for all goods and services are not only in line but also to challenge some vendors to be more aggressive.

The Multiplier

Look at the cost of a plastic tray, for example, and count how many you use per day. Multiply the number of trays per day by the business days in the year, and multiply that number by the cost of a single tray. Then you will know how much money you have spent on trays. Therefore, 12 trays per day x 250 days @ $1.95 per tray = $5,850. If you can figure out a way to use four less trays per day, you will have $1,950 more in your checking account next year at this time. Amazing, right? Then go down the line with all your other paper products and plastic ware. The more business you do, the more bottom line savings you will discover.

Categories

Some of your costs may be fixed, such as rent, auto payments, and insurance. Many others are controllable. Attention to detail in all areas will provide you with more cash at the end of the year. Examine payroll, linen, trash removal, accounting fees, and, of course, food and beverage costs—anything you pay for on a recurring basis. Shaving 1% here and 1% there can add up to tens of thousands of dollars.

YOUR CATERING LEGACY

Mike Roman was a catering industry visionary. He identified a business need and filled it. While was operating his family's catering business, The Mixing Bowl, Mike realized that caterers needed a consulting and educational resource. He started Catersource before the Internet was popular and communicated with his clients by phone and newsletter.

While I only crossed paths with Mike a few times, one of my oldest clients had more extensive experience with him. He shared this story:

> My wife and I had a fast food restaurant in a university area. Naturally, summers were slower because students—the majority of our customers—went home. We identified picnics and tailgate parties as a new revenue stream and booked quite a few.
>
> One rainy Saturday, we loaded up our one and only truck with picnic food for 150 guests. When we arrived at the event site,

the person who had ordered the food told us to go home because the weather was bad. He said he would reschedule the event, but he was adamant that it just was not happening that day. We were young and inexperienced; we were working without sufficient contracts and had only taken a minimal deposit for that event.

Needless to say, I was extremely aggravated, and I remembered there was a guy in Chicago who called himself a catering consultant. His name was Mike Roman and I made an appointment to see him. Armed with our printed menus and brochures, I met Mike in his office. I quickly got to the point of my visit, explained the recent problem with the bad weather day picnic, and asked what we could do to avoid this in the future. Mike immediately told us that our minimal deposit policy was one of the causes of our difficulties, but he went further.

He said that there were three kinds of caterers—shallow, medium, and deep—and frankly, at that point, we were shallow caterers. Mike then explained that with our quality menus and our knowledge of the catering business, we could become deep caterers, and he outlined a strategy for us. After we had mastered picnic catering, we decided to sell our restaurant and become serious corporate caterers.

Again I contacted Mike, and he helped us create a menu and a marketing plan that helped us get beyond the magic $1 million sales mark. I will never forget, at our first meeting, Mike said, "Now I hope neither of you are in love with food, because if you are, you are in the wrong business. Corporate caterers sell time, not food. Your job is to provide a service, and you can never be late." This bit of wisdom stayed with me for years."

Sometimes words like Mike's can be wake-up calls, as we all need to remember the fundamental goals of our sometimes complicated businesses.

I recently had a client tell me, "Michael, I've come to realize that decent food delivered on time is better than exceptional food delivered late." Think about that the next time you spend hours making a sauce from scratch.

Documenting Your Systems =
CONSISTENCY

Consistency =
REPEAT BUSINESS

Repeat Business =
SUCCESSFUL CATERING COMPANY

I am a strong advocate of employees being cross-trained. If scheduling dictates that two different people make tuna salad, there should be a written recipe, so every customer's sandwich looks and tastes the same. Decide how much mayonnaise, salt, pepper, celery, and whatever else you include goes into each portion of tuna.

- Next, put it in writing.

- Next, put it in a three-ring binder in a plastic sheet protector, or post it in the kitchen.

- Make it clear that the recipe is to be followed to the letter. There can be absolutely no individual discretion.

- Next, repeat with every item you produce.

Yep . . . it's a lot of work. No one said it would be easy.

Feeling Overwhelmed?

I've always had a backup plan. *If this catering thing doesn't pan out,* I told myself about 20 years ago, *I'll write a* New York Times *bestselling novel and award the movie rights to the highest bidder.* (Notice, I did not indicate it was a realistic backup plan).

I always enjoyed writing but wanted to learn more about some of the rules of the trade. I signed up for a class, "The Basics of Writing Your First Novel." The first day, the instructor said, "I'm going to go around the room, and I want to hear how people think they become writers."

"I find inspiration while sitting on a pristine beach on a cloudless day," Michaela offered. "I do my best writing in coffee shops on rainy Saturdays," said Luke. After everyone had spoken, it was the instructors turn. "I'm going to tell you the only piece of information you will ever need about how you can become a published writer," he said.

We held our collective breath.

"You sit your ass down in a chair, and you write."

"Because I wield power over others, I am at great risk of acting like an insensitive jerk."

WE ALL NEED HELP

A long time ago, I figured out the best way to accomplish something that I had limited knowledge of was to hire an expert in that particular field. When I began creating menus, I hired a graphic designer with menu experience. When I decided to start a membership website for corporate catering, I hired a web developer. When I started teaching seminars before large groups, I hired a public speaking coach. It works.

If you aspire to start a corporate drop-off/delivery division and don't know where to begin, or if you are a seasoned veteran who wants to take your business to the next level, *we are the experts to contact.* Whether it's templates and downloads to help organize and manage your day-to-day operation, private coaching (including menu creation and sales strategy), on-site consulting, or custom catering leads to generate new business, The Corporate Caterer has a proven track record of success.

Remember, the joy is in the journey. We are available to co-pilot your journey.

For more information, please visit www.TheCorporateCaterer.com, email michael@thecorporatecaterer.com, or call our office (781) 641-3303.

EPILOGUE

A few years after my unforgettable morning with Annie/Agent X, I ran into her, ironically, in a McDonalds. I don't know how we recognized each other, but we did. After a quick exchange of pleasantries, we turned to leave.

I stopped and turned around.

"Annie," I called out.

"Yes?"

"I want to share a quick story that I think you'll appreciate.And I definitely have you to thank because I remember thinking about you as it was unfolding."

"OK."

"First, I need to say for the record that I **don't** do this anymore. It was one thing in my younger, more care-free days, but it's not the kind of example I can set anymore."

"Umm, OK," she said, sounding intrigued and confused.

"On occasion, when I was returning from a tasting that I'd just done, I'd find myself behind a competitors vehicle. (Note: I'd be in my own "unmarked" vehicle). The first time it happened, I heard your voice saying, 'Let's tail his ass, and see where this joker is delivering to.'"

She gasped, and her eyes bulged with excitement.

"So, one day I in fact followed one of these vans as it pulled into an office park that we had never delivered to. I, well . . . sort of got out of my car and loosely followed the driver into the building . . . and kind of caught a glance of the name of the company he was delivering to (from the labels on the trays) . . . and well, about a week after that, I sent them a menu, and then we set up a tasting. And, now they are regular customers of ours.

"Oh my God! O H M Y G O D!" she shrieked, literally jumping and down.

After a minute, she caught her breath, narrowed her eyes and asked in an investigator's tone, "Were you REALLY thinking about me while you were doing that?"

"The whole time, Annie/Agent X. The whole time."

TESTIMONIALS

"The Corporate Caterer's Leads Program WORKS! My sales team is used to spending lots of time prospecting for new catering business. Not anymore. We bought our first Leads List in July, two more in August, and four more in September. Now, instead of spending half their time cold-calling, my sales reps are doing what they do best...Selling!"

Scott
City Kitchen,
Fort Worth, Texas

"The Corporate Caterers LEADS PROGRAM is incredible. No more cold calling! They do all the "grunt work." The first Leads List we purchased generated over $20,000 in new catering business in less than 3 months!"

M. Ricarte
Via Lago Café & Catering
Boston, MA

"Well, lead #1 was lighting rod! I have a lunch tomorrow for the president of the hospital and 20 of his department chairs and their secretaries. Go The Corporate Caterer!

The thing I am most excited about is that we've done catering at different departments, so hopefully there will be some recognition during the tasting that will help secure our reputation with the others that are unaware of us.. I think this could potentially go our way!"

Craig Mosmen
Owner, The Couch Tomato
Philadelphia, PA

Michael Rosman is professional and approachable. He has really taken the time to get to know our goals as a business and I feel confident in the strategies he's helped us develop to achieve those goals. After only a few months we've already seen an increase in our corporate catering business. His humor and experience has been a true asset to my growth as a sales person and I believe the investment we've made with The Corporate Caterer has already, and will continue to pay off.

Ruth Hedges
Sales Associate, Gance's Complete Catering
Binghamton, NY

I am helping to grow a catering division in a family's restaurant. Having no prior experience in catering sales, I needed help. My search stopped when I found Michael's website. I ended up printing the pages and putting them in a 3-ring binder. I refer to it almost daily.

Later, I signed up for his consulting services. Michael is very knowledgeable and professional consultant. He listens, gives great advice and lots of encouragement. He helps me avoid many mistakes. I am more confident each time we have a discussion. It's been only three months, but I am already bringing in new business, and feel that I am moving in a right direction.

Iryna Zaritsky
Catering Sales Manager
MGM Roast Beef Catering

I have been looking for a clear direction in my businesses, owning an off-premise catering company for over 10 years and now a restaurant has not been an easy task. Michael has helped me achieve clarity and supported me in making big decisions to do what's best for my business. With his expertise, he is really helping me build the foundation for my companies so I can grow them on the right path. His direction towards the results I desire are very to the point and compassionate.

Thank you Michael for your support and I am looking forward to keep working together!

Marita Lynn
Marita Lynn Catering & RUNA Restaurant
Aberdeen, New Jersey

We are now in our 37th year of a restaurant AND catering service who specialize in drop off catering. We do many orders per day and specialize in breakfast, lunch and dinner buffets. We deliver all throughout the Chicago land area.

If anything, after reviewing your materials, it has reaffirmed that we are on target with our approach to growth and our day-to-day retention of customers.

As an instructor in a hospitality department of a local Jr. College, I will refer your company to my students so they can use you as a source when they start restaurants and food service operations in the future.

Paul McKenna
Starship Catering
Chicago, Ill

"Michael, to tell you the truth I love your site! It is really useful for a catering company. I love your templates. They are very useful in formatting an operation. Thanks and keep up with your wonderful work!

Marcelo Politi
Nove Eventos
San Pueblo, Brazil

The information provided is amazing. It's organized was very well thought out and I can see the benefits of using your service!

Don P.
Rawstachio
NY, NY.

"Everyone and anyone in the catering business can benefit from joining the Corporate Caterer! This is the most well written informative website in the industry. They cover many various subjects that we all deal with being in this business and it is a great resource to know they are there. Michael is amazing and offers us110% in his customer service. The leads program is absolutely amazing. If I was to hire someone to qualify these leads I would spend well over the amount they charge us. Sometimes it can take 50+ phone calls before you even get one lead...and who has the time for that? His low monthly membership rate is affordable for everyone and well worth it!"

L. Rizzo
Distinctive Tastes
North Shore, MA

"I would like to thank Michael for our recent coaching hour. It is helping me grow the corporate catering end of the catering company I work at. I am a recent executive chef now in the sales office and this is a whole new venture and Michael's techniques have been helping. I would high recommend his personal coaching to anyone. Bon Appetit,"

Christine M. Todaro
Cozy Caterers
Providence, RI

"Thank you so much!

Great website!"

Andree Kosak
Trumps Catering
Athens, Georgia

"Mike was down to earth and very knowledgable about the business of corporate drop off catering. It was absolute pleasure to talk with someone who had experienced some of the same things I am as my business expands. City Kitchen Catering will definitely be seeking his consultation in the future."

Bob Orem
City Kitchen Catering
Philadelphia, Pa

"I have had the true pleasure of speaking with Michael Rosman of the Corporate Caterer over the phone a number of times and I want to say that he is very professional, really knows the corporate catering world very well, but above all, he is a very warm and friendly guy! He is extremely approachable and spends as much time as needed on advice and tips. We have just begun our corporate catering division and I love the monthly pdfs he puts out. I have printed out many of them and use them for reference. Michael's website was the launching pad I needed when I was only thinking of going ahead with this division of my company. I'm so happy it's there. Thank you!"

Davii Mandel
Mi Chicas Catering & Events
Spring Valley , NY

"I ended up hiring Michael to help me create a manual for my catering operation, and things took off from there. Now, we have systems, formulas and procedures for everything. My one-year subscription paid for itself with our very first catering order!"

K.S. Dewey
Dominoes Pizza
Bethesda, MD
New York, NY
Philadelphia, PA

"I am very pleasured with the consultation provided by The Corporate Caterer. Michael Rosman has the perfect mix of knowledge and real world experience. He asked the right questions to understand my needs and had great ideas on how to achieve my goals."

Yasmin Tyebee
Top Nosh Café
San Jose, CA

"We've been in business for over 25 years and corporate catering is another source of revenue to enhance our family's business. Micheal's insight on how to grow our catering operations was extremely helpful. He mentioned things that either I've overlooked or didn't even consider. Details that will make a difference to our bottom line.

It's one thing to read articles or books about how to enhance your business but when you have one-on-one counseling, someone specifically providing applications geared towards your business, it is invaluable. Thank you!"

LaTanya Holland
Lefty's BBQ
Washington, DC

"As an owner of a Pizzeria, I wanted to start offering catering services to the local college and businesses. But frankly, I had no idea where to begin. First, I had to learn some of the basic principles of drop-off catering, such as what to charge for delivery, how many plates and napkins to include with an order, and how to set-up an invoicing system. I tried searching different websites but it was more confusing than helpful.

Finally, I found The Corporate Caterer. It was everything I'd been looking for, all bundled together. I ended up hiring Michael to help me create a manual for my catering operation, and things took off from there. Now, we have systems, formulas and procedures for everything. My one-year subscription paid for itself with our very first catering order!"

K.S.
Dewey Washington, DC

"I joined The Corporate Caterer two months ago. The cost was so reasonable, I thought, "What do I have to lose?" I was amazed at the wealth of user-friendly resources and information. And I like the way the material is organized – a dedicated monthly topic that helps me focus on a specific area of my business.

Honesty, I have learned more from your site in two months than I have from more than ten years of conferences and workshops! As an experienced operator, I did not expect to have so many "Aha! moments" as I read through all the material. I only wish i had found you a long time ago. You have exceeded my expectations as a "Caterer who Delivers Solutions." Thank you, The Corporate Caterer."

Marsha Gayle
Providence, Rhode Island

"Michael Rosman is the ultimate professional. His private coaching is helping me launch my corporate catering division. Michael is patient, immensely knowledgable and to-the-point. Why re-invent the wheel when you have access to Michael's experience. If you are want to grow a corporate catering division, you can't go wrong with Michael and The Corporate Caterer."

Carlton Brown, Chef Owner
Occasional Occasions by Carlton
Atlanta Georgia

31042971R00083

Made in the USA
San Bernardino, CA
29 February 2016